# NEW NORMAL
## Working From Home and Loving It!

By S. Charlebois

Serial Entrepreneur

Stay at Home Parent

## CANADIAN EDITION

ISBN: 9780995246317

Published By Rush Essentials

June 2020

**Eh! Welcome to the new normal in Canada**, where getting *out 'n about* ain't what it used to be and neither is doing business.

The new social dynamic has given rise to the work from home with your kids under foot business culture. It's tempting to plant your bum on the chesterfield and cry all over your maple syrup pancakes and back bacon while washing it down with a 2-4 instead of a double double. None of us would call a penalty for it either. The rest of us Canucks are right there with you in some shape or form.

At some point you're going to have to put some serious thought into rubbing some loonies together and figure out a plan to make more.

Are you new to the world of working from home and being your own boss? Are you stoked by the idea or is it causing a kerfuffle in your work / home balance?

Well hang on to your tuque because you're about to discover secrets to finding your niche, having a solid game plan, and given'r all you got!

**It's time to get at 'er !**

# DEDICATION

I really want to take a moment to thank a few people including my Dad and the many business mentors I have had along the way. A special thanks to my daughter for changing my world in the best way possible.

The privilege of working from home with kids is not for everyone, but I would not have it any other way.

# Table of Contents


Dedication..................................................................................5
Table of Content.......................................................................7
SYNOPSIS ...............................................................................8
ABOUT THE AUTHOR.............................................................9
Chapter 1.................................................................................15
YOU FIRST! ............................................................................15
Chapter 2.................................................................................25
A PLAN.....................................................................................25
Chapter 3.................................................................................31
OPPORTUNITIES ...................................................................31
   1. Selling Your Own Product Versus Being A Representative.
..................................................................................................32
   2. Intellectual Property..........................................................38
   3. SELLING YOUR TIME....................................................48
   4. A BRILLIANT IDEA.......................................................53
Chapter 4 ................................................................................55
OFFICIAL BUSINESS.............................................................55
PART 2  The PIE.......................................................................60
Chapter 5 ................................................................................61
WORKFLOW ...........................................................................61
Chapter 6 ................................................................................68
BRANDING & MARKETING....................................................68
Chapter 7 ................................................................................84
PRODUCTION..........................................................................84
Chapter 8 ................................................................................87
ACCOUNTING & TAXES.........................................................87
Chapter 9 ................................................................................91
DELEGATING...........................................................................91
Chapter 10 ..............................................................................94
OPTIMISING ...........................................................................94
CONCLUSION..........................................................................98
REFERENCE INFORMATION...............................................100

# ABOUT THE AUTHOR

I am no stranger to starting from scratch. Fifteen years ago, at the age of 34, I found myself pregnant, alone and bankrupt. I had to move in with my parents and lick the wounds of a broken marriage while dealing with high risk pregnancy. I had to close my massage center and at that time as a self-employed person I did not qualify for paid maternity. I had no choice but to go on welfare. I was filled with shame, sadness not to mention I was utterly exhausted physically, mentally and emotionally.

I think the one defining character that I pride myself on is my work ethic. There was no way I was going to stay stuck in the system and it was definitely not the example I wanted to set for my daughter.

I used my time on welfare to regroup and regain my strength. I went to counseling to help me deal with postpartum depression and heartbreak. I went back to school and reinvented myself as a gemologist. It was one of my biggest personal accomplishments considering science was never on my radar as a career choice.

Soon I was buying and selling jewelry and gemstones and working as an appraiser for private investors. This career has allowed me to work from home and online for the most part while still providing some amazing adventures around the world.

I have worked in Africa, The Middle East, Asia and all over North America and my clients have been Prime Ministers, Royalty, billionaires, Canadian Border Patrol Service, movie production companies, gemstone & diamond mine owners.  Not bad considering where I was coming from.

I have always been an entrepreneur. I started my first business in high school with my best friend Vicky, we sold junk food to our friends out of an empty locker. In later years I worked for other people on several occasions to get by or to learn new skills but I've just never found that being an employee worked well with my personal needs and lifestyle.

Being my own boss just seemed to be the right fit for me. As my children came along it was even more important for me to have that flexibility in my schedule. My parental goal has always been to be home with my kids. I have been a stay at home / working parent for over 15 years and counting.

For those of you who are finding yourself thrown into this lifestyle due to the current global pandemic situation and are finding it tough, hang in there, I promise it gets better.

Since high school I have written hundreds of business plans and have made every mistake in the book. You name it, I tried it! Multi-level marketing, get rich quick programs, the latest online funnel marketing... I always come back to the same thought, "How can I make this simple and easy to manage?"

This book is about how I simplified my life by simplifying my thinking and how that applies to my business and home life balance.

So, why me and why now? Is the question I asked myself before setting out to write this book in 24 hours (yes, 24 hours. I'll explain later in the chapter about workflow).

My best answer is, we are living in very uncertain times and people around the world are desperate to earn a living in a new stay at home economy forced on us by the Covid-19 pandemic. With supply chain disruptions and no clear end to social distancing, businesses are having a hard time staying afloat. Layoffs are here and now is not the time to just wait it out.

For the last few months I have watched the world around me go mad while my world has stayed relatively intact (at least at the time of writing this book, June 2020). Like everyone I have gone through moments of panic and fear, exhaustion and uncertainty but not to the same degree as many of my friends have. My secret is that I have created an automated system that provides multiple streams of income. This has allowed me to maintain my financial stability.

I will admit that I am not rich. I am more of an example of what not to do and less of a business superstar guru despite my little brag session a couple of paragraphs ago.  I am okay with getting by, especially now. I know I'm really not selling myself here but I think it is important to be honest.

If this pandemic has shown me anything it is that it's not all about big money and the high-life. I have many friends with multi-million dollar corporations or high paying executive jobs and huge homes wondering how they are going to survive the next six months. They are struggling to keep their businesses alive and afford the huge mortgage and car payments. This is creating an enormous amount of stress and upheaval in their lives. With no buyers for big homes the ability to liquidate is quickly becoming a non-option. Foreclosures and bankruptcy is right around the corner for many business gurus and it's nobody's fault.

I am not rich in terms of stock, bonds, corporate salary etc.… I am rich in time, flexibility, versatility, and I have a steady cash flow through good times and bad. If this sounds nice to you right now then keep reading. Who knows you might love being your own boss and do very well at it. In this changing economy, the winners will be the ones who can adapt quickly and address the real world needs of their communities.

My business income comes from a variety of intellectual property, consumable goods, and professional services. Combine that with my relatively small cost of living compared to my lifestyle. I would say I have a winning formula. Part of the reason why I have been able to make this all work is that I have a set of skills and habits that are perfect for the uncertain times that we are living in. I will be sharing those with you as we progress through each chapter.

At the heart of my business is a strong set of principles that are the foundation of everything. From the type of project I take on, the quality of my work, and clients I am lucky enough to work with. Those principles are key for me.

- **Provide Value.** It is important to get paid for my work but I also think it is important that my work be high quality and of value to those who pay for it.
- **Respect & Gratitude.** I respect people's ideas, time, money and their right to take their business to someone else. I also understand that all people are just people first, regardless of how much or how little they can pay me. I am grateful for the work that I receive and humbled when my clients refer me to new clients. If the project is interesting and aligns with me, then I go for it. If not, I walk away. It is not fair to take a client's money if you are not into their project or are not qualified to do it right.
- **Serve the greater good.** I try my best to make the world a better place with the smallest gestures in the present moment and aligning myself with clients whose projects serve a greater good. Being able to improve the world, even in a little way is always worthwhile.

In the spirit of my principals, my goal is to provide you with valuable real world solutions that apply to the situation you might be finding yourself in right now. A situation where self employment from home is your best or only option. Welcome to my world! I never want to go back to the old 9-5 drudge fest.  I welcome the new normal business environment and I hope this book helps to make your transition a little easier.


If you are interested in contemplating your own principles and how you can apply them to your business I recommend the book **Principles by Ray Dalio**.

# Chapter 1

# YOU FIRST!

### Your Business Your Way

Why do you want / need to be an entrepreneur? And what objectives does your business have to meet in order for it to be the right opportunity for you?

Let me give you an example from my own life.

I am a huge reader and more than a few years ago I read the book **Multiple Streams of Income** by Robert G. Allen. I fell in love with this idea, it seemed to me like a good way to hedge my risk while keeping my life interesting. It didn't take me long to start putting my energy into multiple small creative projects.

A flexible schedule and financial security is very important to me as a single parent of two. Having time to be with my kids and to work from home has always been my top priority. By creating small bite size projects I could start and finish them fairly quickly without being too disruptive to my home life.

My time, energy level and money situation was already stretched to the max, so I tried to create businesses to be stand alone and automated centers of cash flow. As a result I developed several small niche market products that I sell online.

After doing several of my own products I developed the skills to help other people do the same. As my kids got older I started to make additional income through consulting and selling my business development services.

It might seem by the way I am writing that I had it all figured out and everything went smoothly. I wish that was true but the reality of it is I failed more than I succeeded.

I have had 1 major challenge that has consistently blocked my success and it took me years to get honest with myself about it. It played out in 2 ways:

1. I avoided the tasks I did not enjoy to the point that it created so much anxiety that I became overwhelmed and did not know how to catch up, never mind get ahead. I am a person who needs an environment with little distraction to be able to get anything done. I'm easily distracted and I hate sales. When it was time to focus on the sales aspect of my business I would use every distraction as an excuse to not do what needed to be done.
2. I love marketing and the creativity of developing the products. I could do that all day long - to the point that I would waste my days coming up with brilliant ideas for the

next multi- million dollar business before I even got the first one up and running.

Boy oh boy, it's amazing how I can find a million things to do before making the sales calls, doing my book keeping and tracking my spending. It is my guess that you will discover similar issues about yourself as well. They may not be the same as mine, but I bet that you will have to face the avoidance and procrastination demon at some point. I highly recommend reading **The Power of Now: A Guide to Spiritual Enlightenment** by Ekart Tolle. It was and still is one of my favorite books. I make a point of reading it again from time to time.

I have seen many businesses fail despite all the enthusiasm in the world. I have seen entrepreneurs invest all of their savings into their dreams only to come out the other end defeated and broke.

**The key to the success of any business is YOU** and how well you know your authentic self. Many people dream of being self-employed and running their own show. They dream of riches, lifestyle and that sense of accomplishment that comes with success. The truth is most people fail over and over again before they make it. I am no exception. To be an entrepreneur who succeeds you have to be prepared to do the things you hate and are not good at. At least at first.

You also have to accept failure as part of the process. The fastest ways to learn is to try and fail, then adjust and try again, and continue until you have mastered the skill.

That is not to say you have to do everything blind and without guidance. I highly recommend finding mentors and getting in the habit of reading daily on the subjects you struggle with most. **The Power of Habit** by Charles Duhigg, was suggested to me by a dear friend and mentor who shall rename nameless. This friend is a highly disciplined person who is always optimizing his habits. Every time he gets new information about how to improve his health, his workflow etc.. he makes a real effort to integrate it into his routine. It is definitely working for him. He has more stamina at 74 years old than men half his age and he is a business powerhouse.

In home based entrepreneurship there are many hats to wear such as researcher, basic accounting, purchasing agent, project developer, application writer, inventory management, web designer, branding, marketing and the list goes on and on. You are never going to be good at all of it so just get that notion out of your head asap. You will burn yourself out trying to do it all. Just the same, as a business owner you do need a solid understanding of everything that goes on and has to happen in order for your business to grow and thrive.

At some point you are going to need help, but in the short term mentors and good books are invaluable. They are like loving encouraging parents teaching you how to walk. They hold your hand until you can find your own balance. They encourage you to keep trying until it becomes natural for you to walk on your own two feet. With practice and determination walking turns into running with confidence.

The very first place to start your business is to turn the focus on to you and your lifestyle goals. Next you will have to be honest about your strengths and weaknesses. You should evaluate your resources of time, money and energy. Not to mention identifying the skills you bring to the table that will benefit your business. Knowing your cost of living will also be very important for when you are trying to determine if a specific plan can meet your needs.

It is easy to get super excited about a great idea but before you go crazy with enthusiasm about your future business, take some time to discover your personality along with your strengths and weaknesses.

I suggest taking the Myers-Briggs TEST. All MBA Students are required to take it

https://www.myersbriggs.org/my-mbti-personality-type/mbti-basics/

This test will help you to figure out things like whether or not you are an introvert or extrovert. What type of decision maker you are and how you interact with the world. Based on your answer you will be given a list of careers and jobs that work well with your personality type.  Finding that right job is so important for your overall satisfaction. When you enjoy what you do it fosters more patience and perseverance. In my opinion those are the traits that lead to success in business. ***STICKTOITIVNESS!***

As humans we all have the same **8 Fundamental Human Needs** that often get overlooked when it is time to plan your business. They are known as **Maslow's Hierarchy of Needs**.

I believe that when these core needs are not properly met in the right priority, we burnout faster. Those 8 needs are:

- Subsistence.
- Understanding and growth.
- Connection and love.
- Aesthetic.
- Contribution.
- Esteem and Identity.
- Self-governance (Autonomy).
- Significance and purpose.

To learn more about Maslow's Hierarchy of Needs, you can visit: https://www.simplypsychology.org/maslow.html

The question that you need to ask yourself is:

**"What 3 do I need most?"**

Famed author and motivational coach, Anthony Robbins often talks about this in his seminars where he shows the correlation of these needs and how it impacts your most intimate relationships. I think of a business as a personal relationship, and believe it has a direct impact on our overall work satisfaction.

Your business and home life will need to be able to provide all 8 needs in order for you to continue to take interest in it and to push yourself to succeed but if your top 3 needs are not met as the underlying purpose, your success could be short lived.

It might seem obvious that we all need subsistence met as our number 1 but actually for many, this might be the least important for feeling fulfilled and happy.  Everyone's a little different and that is perfectly fine.

**My top 3 needs are:**

**1. Self-governance** -This actually helps me meet my need for connection in the way that I can have quality time with my kids.

**2. Subsistence** - In terms of regular steady income to cover the cost of our basic needs. I would rather have a slow steady stream of cash flow than to have many highs and lows that you can find in seasonal work or big ticket sales.

**3. Understanding and Growth** - I love to learn and challenge my ideas otherwise I get bored. I prefer simple quick start-up projects that I can automate over larger multifaceted projects that may take years to implement fully, like in large scale manufacturing or real estate development.

There are many free online surveys that you can take that will help you to determine the priority of your 8 needs. It is well worth the time it takes to really find out, you might be surprised by the results. I know I was.

I am a very adventurous person and an avid outdoor enthusiast. I pride myself on being happy with very few material things and my life's dream is to live off grid and have a permaculture farm in the summer while traveling all winter. I was surprised to find out how important stability really is to me and what it represents. Because of my health issues, and kids schedules, maintaining a steady income has at times been a challenge to maintain.  When I became a parent, that anxiety grew. By knowing this, I have taken it into consideration and built my business around the concepts of passive income through dividend, royalties and steady long term contract work. I can easily work around my daily state of health and hectic family schedule from any location and my monthly income remains relatively stable.

Since making this shift in my thinking, my business objectives have become more focused and decision making and taking targeted action is easier with better results. The clearer the objective in your mind's eye the easier it is to attract opportunities to you and the faster you can take action on them.

Taking the time to really know what you need from your business and identifying your strengths and weaknesses will help you avoid a lot of mistakes caused by oversights and over enthusiasm.

By knowing who you are you can tailor your work-life to your strengths and compensate for your weak spots. Let me give you an  example, I love teaching science and art, they come naturally to me and I really enjoy spending time doing this type of work, so I created a business that is centered on exactly that. I hate sales and accounting so I have learned to automate my sales and commit a few limited hours every week to monitoring and managing my accounting and finances.

Developing the RIGHT discipline can take years when you are focused on the wrong things for you. By knowing what you don't like to do, tells you right away what you need to concur. By breaking the unpleasant aspect of work into manageable bite size tasks and creating a workflow routine, these tasks do not become a scary monster of a job that you want to hide from.

The game changer happened for me when I stopped avoiding my authentic self. I stopped trying to create someone else's idea of success and started working with my priorities, strengths and weaknesses.  Some thing I learned from Devina Kaur, the author of TOO **FAT** TOO **LOUD** TOO **AMBITIOUS**: A SEXY BRILLIANT HAND BOOK

By facing the stuff we don't like to do we actually empower ourselves and it lightens the anxiety and guilt that can come with procrastination. The tendency to avoid the things we are not good at is normal, most people have issues with this in at least one area of their life. I would say that facing the things you do not like or are not good at is the one skill that will help you the most in your career as a business owner.

# Chapter 2

# A PLAN

### A Good Plan Is The Best Plan

I don't want to take the wind out of your sail. I know you probably have a hot idea that you are just dying to jump start. I realize that it is an AMAZING idea or your life dream or the next trend... I have been there. I have been a millionaire in my mind more times than I can count. If only I had... (fill in the blanks)

Or maybe you are at a loss, you are broke or going broke fast and you need to do something quick before you get buried in debt or worse, bankruptcy. The problem is you have no clue what you can do, where to start and how to make it happen. I've been there too. My best advice is breathe, don't panic. You will get through this one step at a time. I believe in you!

The thing with ANY business idea is that it needs to be based or realistic and achievable objective. To do that, your business needs structure and focus that comes from insight. That takes time, energy and/or money.

My dad taught me young how to develop a business plan and why it is so important. This skill has saved me millions of dollars and years of my life that I might have wasted chasing empty dreams.

At first I really hated doing them because I was in a hurry to get started and I found the process of developing a business plan tedious. I was also doing them with the wrong intention. I used to start these documents with the idea of finding funding from banks or potential investors. Then I gave up on doing them all together because I was financing my own projects. I soon realized that a business plan is **ALWAYS** the right place to start.

Before spending a penny, this should be considered your **No. 1 Business Asset! A business plan** will help you to discover what the real costs of doing business are going to be. Things you will discover should include:

- The type of business registration you need, eg. sole proprietorship, limited liability partnership,  incorporation. You can find this information on your provincial business registry website of on the Government Of Canada site: https://www.canada.ca/en/revenue-agency/services/tax/businesses/topics/registering-your-business/business-registration-online-overview.html
- Your mission statement and the core principles. There are plenty of business sites on the web that can guide you in making a powerful mission statement.

- Identifying and calculating your start up costs. These are everything you need and pay for in order to deliver a quality product or service in a professional manner.
- Unit costs or hourly rate.
  - I like to follow freelancer Jenifer Bourn at https://jenniferbourn.com/calculate-freelance-hourly-rate/
  - BC Open Textbooks https://opentextbc.ca/principlesofaccountingv2openstax/chapter/calculate-predetermined-overhead-and-total-cost-under-the-traditional-allocation-method/
- Running cost (recurring monthly and annual fees such as web hosting, equipment repair, salaries or contractors fee…)
- Your potential profit margins, (how much of your sale is left after everything is paid)
- Your sales goals (the amount you need to sell to make it all worth your time and effort)
- Who your competition is and what % of the market you need to capture to take your place. A key questions you need to ask are:
  - Can you compete?
  - Do they have the power to sink you before you start swimming?
- Identifying your target market.
  - Can they afford you?
  - Do they need or want your product?

- Are they willing to spend their hard earned money on it?
- Identifying potential hurdles such as:
    - Trade marking
    - Legal liabilities
    - Specialty insurance
    - Skills development
    - Supply chain...
- Who you need to hire to do what. What are all the things you hate doing or that you need help with?
- How much capital will you need to raise? Can you qualify for financing through a traditional bank or do you need to find venture capital and what's that going to cost you in interest and what are the terms of the loan?
- How long will it take to break even? **How long can you eat shit for before you start to see some light, do you have what it takes to push through the grind?**

According to the BDC.ca
https://www.bdc.ca/en/articles-tools/entrepreneur-toolkit/templates-business-guides/pages/business-plan-template.aspx

Your business plan should include

1. Business overview: A brief description of your company and where it stands in the marketplace;

2. Sales & marketing plan: The sales & marketing strategies that will be used to target your customers;
3. Operating plan: A description of the physical aspect of your business operations;
4. Human resources plan: Details on your key staff, HR policies & procedures;
5. Action plan: The planned actions of the business over the next 2 to 3 years;
6. Executive summary: A summary of the reasons you are seeking financing, together with a summary of your business operations;
7. Financial appendix: The facts and figures that back up what you say in your plan.

There are plenty of great sites online to help you build a stunning business plan but there is no need to go all in right away.

More important than what is included in your business plan to entice potential financing is how it can help you to decide if your plan is viable in the first place. Then you have to ask yourself if you are the right person for the job of bringing this business to life.

I may have written hundreds of business plans but I did not act on most of them. Not all of my ideas were great on paper while others required too much of me for the business to be a good fit for my lifestyle.

In the beginning of my entrepreneurial career I would try to convince people of my AMAZING idea before I convinced myself. This proved to be a costly mistake. I was too lazy to do the business plan, now I am too lazy to start a business without one.

The way I do a business plan is in 3 drafts.

**The 1st draft** is for you to convince yourself. It does not need to be pretty or professional, it just needs to answer some key questions.

1. Is there market demand?
2. Who is your competition?
3. Is there enough profit margin to make it worth your while?
4. What about this idea excites you?

**The 2nd draft** is to address the obstacles

1. What's it going to cost in terms of time, money and expertise?
2. Am I qualified to handle the commitment?
3. Can I do it better than the competition?
4. Is there room in the market for me?
5. What am I missing in terms of time, money and skill and how will I fix that?
6. Do I see myself doing what it takes to get this up and running and is this the business for me?

**The 3rd  and final draft** should not only be a document that you can present to investors but also a guide for future decision making. A plan of action for all areas of your business. In this copy you will create and include the **3 beacons.** They are:

1. **Your mission statement** and guiding principles, they will help your decision making process.
2. **List of assets** that are part of the business, this includes your talent, experience, tools of the trade, and influence. This will help you to know your worth as a company.
3. **Your 1, 3 and 5 year objectives**. These should keep you pointed in the direction of the opportunities you seek.

Things changing is the nature of life, that is why it's good to update and review where you are with your business goals. I make it a regular practice to review my business plans every year to measure my results and to hold myself accountable for those results.

# Chapter 3

# OPPORTUNITIES

**There Are Opportunities Everywhere.**

Outlined here are some simple business ideas that are fairly straight forward and low cost to start. With each business structure you will need different skills and tools. I will do my best to point you in the right direction and give you food for thought to help you in narrowing down which type of business might be best for you.

# 1. Selling Your Own Product Versus Being A Representative.

### MANUFACTURING

I manufacture a cosmetic product called Hand Jam Callus Care. It caters to a niche market and has slowly started moving towards the mainstream population thanks to word of mouth and the magic of social media.

Hand Jam was born from my need for something that would help my hands after rock climbing. I worked in the cosmetic industry at the time and so I made myself a batch of blended oils that really worked. Soon I was sharing it with fellow climbers. Before long small local gyms, convenience stores close to outdoor climbing areas and outdoor retailers started carrying Hand Jam and it has developed a cult like following in a niche market of rock climbers. Due to social isolation we have made it available on Etsy and Amazon.

This simple little product has now supplemented my income since 2002 with almost no effort on my part in the last 10 years. I have low overhead, a simple production set up and the shipping and sales are all automated. This business model is based on developing repeat clients who are loyal to the brand. By identifying with the climbing community, I am able to tap into and genuinely understand the need for quality callus care. My training in cosmetology and experience as an educator with one of leading hand and foot care companies in North America, Creative Nails, gave me the added credibility over the artisanal beeswax salves producers. My product is unique in formulation and is specifically made for maintaining flexible callus. Please bear with me, I am bragging to make a point.

I was able to create a simple, effective product that added value to its target market. I was able to build rapport with my client and establish credibility. The production is simple and about 75% automated. The best part is the profit margins are healthy and the consumable nature means repeat business. One client = Multiple sales over time.

Cosmetic manufacturing is big business and if you are thinking about going this route you need to follow some specific rules. Be sure to check with Health Canada for current regulations and guidelines that apply to ingredients, product declaration, packaging and labeling. https://www.canada.ca/en/health-canada/services/consumer-product-safety/cosmetics/notification-cosmetics.html Most manufactured products, not just cosmetics need to follow various guidelines. Here are some typical guidelines that you might need to look into before you start selling your product.

- Canadian label laws
- Product declaration that will require a list of ingredients
- Packaging Standards
- Shipping Restrictions
- Expiration Dates
- Liability Disclaimers
- Liability Insurance
- Bar-code Generation & Product Registration (GS1 Canada)
- Material Safety Data Sheet (USA)

This list is my no means complete. You will have to do your own research. There are many great resources for information such as Health Canada. I will be including a list of resources at the back of this book for easy reference. It is important to do your homework if you are going to be manufacturing and selling a product in Canada. There are liability issues to consider, and possible additional costs of liability insurance. In the case of cosmetics you can not sell in big box stores without this insurance. There are also shipping restrictions when selling in the US on all liquid items. If you are not sure what rules will apply to you it is best to consult with a variety of professionals within the field you want to work in. I have found most people are willing to share their knowledge when they know you are starting out in business. Establishing a good network of colleagues early on can be a huge advantage for you and your business.

Why I like cosmetic products is that you are selling a consumable product with healthy profit margins. Once you are able to organize your production line and quality control it is an easy business to automate by using drop shipping services. You make a large batch, ship it to the warehouse and let them handle the distribution.

Seller Central / Amazon.ca  are the perfect example of a user friendly platform that is designed to help you find your clients and get your product into their hands. From your Amazon dashboard, you can monitor sales, inventory and even promote. It is an all in one solution for simple start up ideas. Another sell site I have used and gotten good results with was Etsy.

Food Production is a very similar business model but because of the shelf life issues, this is less of an option for someone like me, but for the right person it can be an excellent opportunity.

Producing your own product can be something as simple as sewing masks or something more involved like making wire wrap jewelry like my friend Shelly from Shelly's Stoneworks.  She buys rough gemstone material from me, polishes it and turns them into magnificent tree of life wire wrap pendant that she sells at her Etsy store and at a local market on weekends.

## SALES REPRESENTATIVE

This is my least favorite type of home based business but that does not mean there isn't success to be had with this approach. I hate sales but I totally see the value in a good sales person. There are literally thousands of companies out there that are desperate for a good rep with a sales strategy and a "go get 'em" attitude.

Of course companies like **Avon,  Tupperware** and **Epicure** come to mind. They are good companies with a solid track record and quality product, My cousin Kimberly Smith is a tupperware representative and she is really into it. She makes social media videos that really sell the product in a very human way.

If that sounds a little too vanilla for you don despair. I have one wild funny friend who was making a tidy profit selling sex toys. She had a talent for making the uncomfortable a little less awkward and even fun.

Whatever you are into is what you should be selling and the reason is that it does not take long to blow through your friends and family support network who will buy because they want to encourage you. To really make it in sales you need a market that you can easily connect with.

Being a product rep does not have to be a forever career choice. <u>Louise Forget</u> a dear friend of mine used to sell **Epicure** spices. She is a wonderful cook and loves making great meals for her family. Good food is something she really enjoys. She tried out just about everything she sold, sharing it with friends and family along the way. This side lined bridged the gap while Louise built her art business which is her true passion after her kids.

Whatever you are into is what you should be selling and the reason is that it does not take long to blow through your friends and family support network who will buy because they want to encourage you. To really make it in sales you need a market that you can easily connect with.

Repping can also be an add on to your existing business. Here is an example of another friend of mine who is an avid fitness gym goer. He works out a couple times a week, studied nutrition and works as a massage therapist. He takes vitamins regularly for himself and liked the product so much he decided to make them available to his nutrition and massage clients. The vitamin product line was an easy add on to his at home business.

Things to consider before becoming a product rep is the upfront investment. Many of these companies want you to be your own boss and buy into their box business plan. This investment might look something like a commitment to buy a certain dollar amount of products, or to purchase your starter kit with product samples, sales guide and marketing tools. There may be monthly or annual fees to maintain your dealer status.

In return they provide a quality product that is ready to sell. They usually handle all of the deliveries, and have polished marketing and sales training support. You also benefit from having mentors who have created a level of success in the company and can help you build your business.

I think this is a good option if you like sales, can afford the relatively small startup and are not afraid of the commitment. This option offers a lot of pluses if you don't feel like blazing your own trail.

If you think this could be the solution for you, I suggest you read **How to Sell Anything to Anybody** by Joe Girard in this book you will find strategies to overcome the most common sales issues, and how to close the sale.

# 2. Intellectual Property

This opens the door for creative people on many levels. I personally have 3 different ways that I make money from my intellectual property.

**BOOK PUBLISHING.**

This is my 3rd book and I earn royalties on sales. I self-publish, work with a team of contract editors, and register my books with ISBN Canada https://www.bac-lac.gc.ca/eng/services/isbn-canada/Pages/isbn-canada.aspx. The books are then uploaded onto various platforms where they are made available for print on demand.

Here is a list of what you will need to do to become a published author.

- ISBN Canada
  https://www.bac-lac.gc.ca/eng/services/isbn-canada/Pages/isbn-canada.aspx

- A professional cover that is in line with the genre and suitable for printing (quality graphic design is required).
- A Synopsis. What the book is about in a nutshell.
- Professional picture of you, the author (optional)
- SELL SHEET for dealers and stores purchasing agents, you can easily find templates on line
- A website, either an "Authors page" or a site just for your "Feature" book
- Press releases
- Press Kit
- Social media presence
- You will need a plan for promoting your book eg. being a guest on PODcasts, television and radio. Don't forget social media influencers!
- You will need a professional print and distribution company.  Amazon Kindle and IngramSparks are 2 that are free or affordable for self publishing authors.
- You will need a clearly defined category for your book
- Book review testimonial

There are many companies out there that can help you with your project and handle all of the tedious technical stuff if you are not inclined to go the do it yourself route. These are not your typical publishing houses, they specialize in self-publishing and they can save you a ton of time and greatly improve the quality of your work. By matching you with the right editors and graphic design team they can develop your branding and marketing strategy. They not only give you a professional edge they also walk you through every step of the way. Of course this comes with a $ cost and a big investment of time.

A well written book that caters to a specific niche can generate royalties for many years. My first book, **The Very Sleepy Mouse** is a children's book written with the specific task of getting kids to fall asleep fast. It is based on subliminal messaging, mirroring techniques and guided meditation all disguised as a cute bedtime story. Like **HandJam** this was a product that I needed in my own life and I had the skills and tools to create it, so I did. It started out as a few drawings that I did to go along with the story that my son and I made up together. What my son did not know is that I was using repetitive suggestive words and meditation relaxation techniques on him to bore him to sleep.

After the drawings were made I added the text and made my own print copy. I was so proud of this little project. One day I was bragging to a friend about how it made me feel closer to my boy and we looked forward to bedtime now, not to mention he fell asleep within 7 minutes. She asked me if she could get a copy to give it a try on her daughter. She had a very similar result. After that I gave a few more copies away and started getting great feedback. Next thing I knew I was applying for an ISBN and trying to navigate the world of publishing.

I am confident that I will always have a market of exhausted parents desperate to get their kids to sleep. If nothing else this little pet project taught me what I needed to know about publishing and I have been able to add that to my resume as part of my business knowledge and consulting service.

If publishing a book is a bit too big of a bite, you should try your hand at blogging.

## BLOGGING

The best part about blogging is that the blog remains online as long as you continue to host them so the running cost is basically your time and the web hosting fees. There are blog sites that you can use for free but I prefer to control my platforms.

There are a few tricks to being a successful blogger regardless if you are a ghost writer (writing for someone else under their name) or writing for yourself.

- **Follow a formula** - This will help you to write quickly, with structure and in a coherent fashion so readers can read through to the end with purpose.

- **Google TRENDS** - If it is your own blog then Google Trends is your best friend. Google allows you to search words and phrases that are trending. This will help you to know what is on people's minds in your target market. You can then tailor your work around what people want to read. Blogging is all about relevancy and eyeballs, the more people who read your blog, means the more people who will be exposed to it because it will reach higher in search engine ranking.

- **Learn SEO best practices** - Search engine algorithms create ranking for your content. If goes a lot further than just being relevant. It is also about being unique. Avoid the temptations to copy paste the same blog on different sites. This will actually kill your ranking. SEO specialists are well paid so this is a skill you can develop for yourself and market to other bloggers as well.  Remember to update your knowledge of SEO standards regularly. It changes about every 6 months.

- **Affiliate marketing** - This is a way to promote companies and products within your blog posts. To do affiliate marketing you need to find quality affiliates and you need to know how to make links within your blog. With some very easy basic web design skills you should be able to do this with little stress.

There are 2 common ways that this is done within blogs .

1. The first is to create links out of the relevant keywords that link back to an affiliate company that sells the type of product mentioned. For

example, if you are reading this book in digital form you will notice underlined text highlighted in blue (links) that when clicked on will take you to the web location of that person or product. Every time you click on those links and make a purchase I have the chance to earn a commission on the sale. You can easily do the same by signing up to companies such as Amazon Affiliates or CJ.com to name a few. These sites will generate links for you that contain a visitor tracking code known as cookies.

2. The second way to promote affiliates is to place banner ads at the top, middle and bottom of your blogs. Every time people click on the ads you have a chance to earn money. Mass production bloggers tend to favor this method because people accidentally touch the images while scrolling. Personally I am not a fan. It distracts the reader and bombards them with repetitive ads. These blogs also tend to be 'click bait' in nature. This means they have a catchy thumbnail image and intriguing title but they offer no real value in terms of information.  They are predatory in nature.

- **URL and WEBSITE Hosting** - I use **WIX.com,** there is also Wordpress and many more companies that offer ready made websites templates that require no knowledge of coding or web design.


## GHOST WRITING


You might be surprised to know that I make a considerable income from ghost blogging for other people despite having dyslexia, I love to write and I overcome my challenges by working with  Stephanie Lariviere, from Spellerella's Haven she is so much more than an editor, she and I have a great working dynamic. Having an editor really raises the quality of your work and helps to shape your ideas and bring greater clarity and power to the content.


Avoid writing fluff that gives nothing to the reader or being too formal to the point that the reader can not connect to you as a person. A good blog will develop a following and that happens when the reader sees themselves in your words and can relate on a personal level. Your goal should be to write with authority from your specialized knowledge, the sharing of your thought analysis and your personal stories.


As humans we connect through stories, shared experiences and common goals. So your writing should be empathetic as well as authentic. If you write as an authority on a subject, then you need to be prepared for the challenge of proving your worth. Never assume your readers are somehow beneath you or that you are in some way superior.  This is the fastest way to lose followers. Just because the medium we are using to communicate is cold and impersonal, your words and attitude should not be.

I tend to write with the intent of doing "my part" for the common good by sharing what I have learned so far. This book is the perfect example of that and so is my personal blog "<u>Soap N' Water</u>" that you can find on Facebook or my website <u>suzannecharlebois.com</u>. I genuinely believe that we can all help each other to grow as people and in our awareness of the world around as. If we do this in an empathetic way that comes from relatable experience then that is the best we have to offer.

There are far better writers out there than me so I suggest finding the ones that resonate with you, emulate them and eventually you will find your own style and flow.

By being consistent with your theme, and frequency, you will start to develop a following. Though views are important, the quality of your words and the relevance of your afflliate ads are probably more important. People click on links that interest them.

**ARTWORK, GRAPHIC DESIGN & PHOTOGRAPHY - With print on demand sales options.**

All of my art is available for print and I use several websites including Fine Art America and Dreamstime. They allow artists to upload digital copies of their work. Then people can order framed prints in a variety of sizes and finishes. They can be turned into custom yoga mats, tote bags, pillows etc. This is great service for interior designers and art galleries because you can do limited editions as well. These sites pay you a commission every time someone buys your prints. What's nice about many of these services is that they allow you to control the profit margin. The downside is that there is lots of competition. What can set you apart is having a signature style, being able to do custom design work or tap into niche markets. The upside to print on demand is that you can do the setup once, automate your advertising and let it run. I'll be the first to admit that I have not done too many print sales from these sites, but I have gotten a few very lucrative clients who hired me for one of a kind art piece and branded art to feature with their product lines.

When it comes to art I try to be as versatile as possible, working with various styles, mediums and color pallets. My biggest thrill is working directly with my clients in mind. I love when they become a part of the creative process and my job is to help them bring their vision to life.

Living the artist life is definitely not for everyone but if it is in your soul then you almost have no choice in the matter. In my experience, to do well as an artist you need some discipline and the ability to let go of your creations. This is a challenge for many artists I have worked with, they either lack the drive to do the stuff they don't like or the ability to finish a piece of work because it is never quite right. This is the curse of the starving artist.

I am very blessed to have been able to earn a healthy income from both my graphic design work and my original paintings. The sale of the original paintings tends to ebb and flow and is directly related to how much I put it out there and promoted it. More often than not, my paintings are sold to friends or friends of friends, and the occasional collector. I decided years ago that I would not make painting my life even though I love it. Just the same I get so much joy out of working on a piece of art for a client. It is my favorite thing to do to earn money.

Freelance designers are also very much in demand especially if you have some art theory training to go with your technical skill. Today just about anyone can make a stunning social media post using the apps on their phone, but not everyone has a natural eye for color, balance, and structure. Nowadays, many businesses hire social media specialists who can design branded posts and create compelling content. You can learn this skill quickly and I think you can even find courses for cheap on sites like GROUPON. These groupon courses are enough to get you started and if you like it then it is easy enough to keep growing your knowledge with other online tutorials.

If your thing is photography then you may be able to make a few bucks with stock photos companies. Most of these companies will allow you to upload your photos to their database and when one is sold you are paid your royalties.

# 3. SELLING YOUR TIME

This is by far the easiest thing you can do if you are in a pinch for cash now, but it is often the least lucrative and the least efficient use of your time. That being said if you are social and a hands on person this might be the most enjoyable way for you to make money. It can also be a very simple thing to set up.

- Help people move
- Run errands for seniors
- Delivery person
- Home Painting
- Handy Person
- Lawn Care
- Auto Detailing

Most of these put you in little contact with people so there is low risk in this COVID-19 environment, you are serving the greater needs of your community and you usually get paid on a daily basis in cash.

The best way to find clients is on Facebook Marketplace, Craigslist, local bulletin boards and best of all, word of mouth. When you show up clean, kind, and ready to work and then deliver results, people like that and they are usually more than happy to spread the word. Be sure to have at least 20 business cards on you at all times and don't be shy to ask for referrals. VistaPrint.ca is a great place to order business cards online. The quality is good and the price is fair. Best of all, they deliver quickly. I use my local printer and they keep all of my print work on file so I just need to call them and usually within 24 hours I can pick up my order. I believe now more than ever it is important to shop local and find your own community, and possible a new client for yourself

## SELLING YOUR EXPERTISE

Do you have a unique skill or knowledge that you can teach or offer as a consultant? Perhaps you are a mother of 5 and know exactly how to get your kids to sleep without drugging them or taping them to the bed. Or maybe you make the best cloth diapers in town. There are lots of ways to sell your talent and expertise.

YouTube videos are one way to attract potential customers. They can lead to offering online classes. Hosting a podcast on the subject is another way to reach people.

Again here you will need a little technical skill and a good camera/ microphone but most phones today are more than adequate to start and most hosting platforms are easy to use and understand if you are patient enough to read though the instruction

In these scenarios I have found it helpful to give away for free a little bit of what you know and then invite people to join you for a series of sessions or classes. You can pre-record the classes and let people learn on demand or you can host exclusive live events.

One YouTuber (and published author) whom I have the pleasure of working with is <u>Devina Kaur</u>, the founder of <u>SexyBrilliant.org</u> non profit foundation. Her personal mission is to dispel toxic shame and leads by promoting radical self-acceptance. She recognises that loneliness and heartbreak are a major cause of depression, anxiety, addiction, poor self esteem. Her solution is to offer an online course, <u>The Heartbreak Process</u>, for free to all of her site members. The videos are on her YouTube channel. YouTube allows you to monetize your channel without having to use heavy handed sales techniques on your audience. Monetizing in this instance means that ads are placed within your videos.

If you go the YouTube channel way and hope to monetize your site. You best be prepared to put in a lot of time and work into promoting your channel. In order to qualify, you need a minimum number of followers and you have to have a minimum number of watched hours per year (this changes very often but currently stands at 1000 subscribers and 4000 views).

It is my experience that this comes with time and quality content. Blogging and or video editing is a skill of its own and it requires good storytelling skills and some technical savvy with a video editing software.  There are freelancers who can do this for you for a fee. You can also  learn this skill and sell your talent.

Consultancy work is very much in demand especially when someone is trying to master a new skill. How much would you pay someone to teach you how to retire at 55? Show you how to be a stress free single parent? I bet you would be willing to watch a free YouTube video.

## FLIPPING

This one is self explanatory. You buy something, clean it up and resell it. You can do this with cars, boats, tailors, bikes, antiques ... Your best place to start is in your own garage or with things that you are genuinely interested in. I know people who have started small by collecting scrap metal and then worked their way up to houses and apartment buildings.

Why not take the flipping challenge and get your family involved. Here is how it works; You buy an Item for $1 then sell it for $2. Then you buy your next item for $2 and sell it for $4. 4 to 8, 8 to 16 and so on. In a perfect world you could be a millionaire in just 21 transactions. If you did 1 transaction a week it would take you less than 6 months to go from broke to financial freedom. Of course you can not spend it until you have completed the challenge. That takes discipline!

There are some things you will need to consider if you plan on flipping bigger ticket items such as cars and homes. If you sell more than a certain number of cars in a year then you need a dealership license. So be sure to check your local laws.

For houses, if they are not your principal residence you will have to pay capital gains taxes after deductions. Check with an accountant to know what the tax implications are.

My friend and business associate John Grow from <u>Prestige Evaluation Professional Appraisal Service</u>, is an amateur (HAM) Radio operator and collector. Every year he goes to the local HAM Events and various flea markets. He buys radios, fixes them up and resells them. This little hobby of his is also a nice side gig that he really enjoys and he makes money doing something he would probably do anyway. While at these flea markets he often meets collectors of other things such as antiques, watches, vintage cars, etc. Before long he has found a new client for his professional appraisal service. My point here is, be involved with the community that will buy your products or use your services.

# 4. A BRILLIANT IDEA

**When you just know it's going to be great**

Tell me if this sounds familiar. You have this great idea but you don't want to talk about it too much or in detail because you are afraid someone will steal it or do it before you have a chance to. I have heard this a million times. More often than not someone else gets it out to market before you can because they have access to funding and a team of professionals, or the idea dies because it never got off the ground.

If this is your story, here are some key ways you can protect yourself and your idea and why you really should. To get something out to market quickly takes a team and unless you are Apple or Tesla it is almost impossible to work in secret code. You are going to have to trust and hire people to help you get the job done well. That does not mean you just go around trusting anyone and that you don't take steps to protect yourself. Lawyers, patents, and trademarks can be expensive. The process is tedious if you try to go the DIY (do it yourself) way but it is possible. Chances are you might need to confide in someone before you even get to that stage.

The best way to protect yourself is to have a non competition non disclosure agreement between you and the people you chose to work with. You can include the broad and general description of what it is you are making and have them agree that they will not share or work on similar projects while under contract and for a defined period of time after the end of their contract with you, this includes patenting or trademarking any product that would directly compete with yours. Or working for another company that is developing a similar product that would be in direct competition with yours.

There are plenty of FREE standard NCND's (non competition non disclosure) available online that can be easily modified to suit your needs. Lawdepot.ca is an affordable legal documents service. They really help to cut down on legal fees especially for things like standard contracts. I have used them several times over the years.

You can hire a legal firm to help you with the paperwork and logistics of trademarks and patents but you can also do it yourself for a fraction of the cost directly on the Government of Canada Website at https://www.ic.gc.ca/eic/site/cipointernet-internetopic.nsf/eng/h_wr00002.html

Another cost effective way you can protect your intellectual property is to mail to yourself a copy of your plans, designs and notes via registered mail.  Do not open this envelope and keep it safe in a safety deposit box just in case you ever have to go to court to prove your claim. Keep a duplicate copy of what is in the envelope for your legal counsel so that they can go over the evidence without breaking the seal on the registers envelope. This does not replace patents, trademarks or copyright but it can prove your case for stolen intellectual property.

# Chapter 4

# OFFICIAL BUSINESS

**WHAT TYPE OF BUSINESS ARE YOU AND WHY IT MATTERS.**

My dad used to say, "The Government is always your partner". What he meant by that is they are there to help as long as you play fair and honest.

Forget to pay them or follow the rules and they will turn on you. So instead of stressing over the government, accept that they are part of the equation regardless of the nature and structure of the business.

**Business Registration-**

**Using your own name-** The government website is a great source of information on the different ways you can make your business official and it is worth checking it out.   In many cases you do not need to register a business name at all if you are working under your own legal name.   Eg. John Doe, Bricklayer. You are considered a sole proprietor but you don't have to pay the governments an annual business registration fee.  It is a clean and simple solution.  You do however need to declare all

business income over $2000 ( please check this threshold
amount based on your provinces regulations)

**Having a Unique  Business Name**

**Registered Sole Proprietorship** -How is being Sole Proprietor
with an official business name other than your own different from
working under your own name?  The main difference is that you
get to market your business under an assumed name or a legal
business name  such a  A1 Brick Layers reg.  You have to pay an
annual business registration fee and you are issued a business
number to go with your chosen business name.

This option gives your business its own identity and may make it
more attractive to sell at some point in the future.

You are still personally liable for any losses or lawsuits so you
need to consider that carefully.  What are the risks and liabilities
related to your business.  Do you need special liability
insurance?  Some insurance companies will not insure you if you
are not a certified professional in your field of expertise.

**Limited Liability Partnership.**  This is where partners go into
business together and share the risks and responsibilities as well
as the financial  gains.  Like a registered business each partner is
personally liable and can be sued for damages or responsible for
debt repayment and bankruptcy will be on their personal credit

score.  Again you need to pay an annual business registration fee and prepare and annual financial statements for your taxes.

In this type of set up it is always advisable to have a contract agreement between the partners that outline the individuals roles within the company,  their share percentage and terms for buyout as termination.  Business partnerships can turn best friends into enemies so cross your t's and dot your i's.

**An Incorporation** is a great option when there needs to be a total separation between the person and the business entity. Incorporation needs directors and financial statements prepared by a CPA as part of their annual declaration.  You can incorporate without a lawyer through either your provincial business registry or the Canadian business registry.

Incorporating your company is a great idea when there is a lot of liability such as large loans, risk of malpractice, or theft or financial losses due to damage.  A good example of this is a jewelry store.  Let's imagine that a client's 100 year old 3 carat diamond ring got lost, stolen or damaged while in your care and the client decided to sue you.  You better hope you have insurance and that you are incorporated.

This prevents the client from going after your personal assets. Just be sure to check the current laws.  In some cases the officers of the company may be liable in a court case against the company.  Example would be if the company is found guilty of dumping toxic waste, committing consumer fraud, known manufacturing defects that lead to bodily harm.  I am not sure to what extent the law applies.  It is always best to consult with a corporate lawyer to understand your real risks and obligations as an officer of the company.

**Other official government  things you will need to take care of:**

**Sales Tax**- If you go this route you need to be careful when it comes to collecting sales taxes.  If your sales are under a certain threshold you are not obligated to collect sales tax.  Be sure to check with your province to know what that threshold number is.

**Employees** - If you plan on having employees then you will need an employer number.  You will be governed by fair wage laws, equal opportunity practices, responsible for wage deductions, such as unemployment contribution, health insurance…. to get the right advice for your province, it is best to consult an accountant, payrolls, specialist and or government services, that can provide you with the most up to date rules and regulations.

**Contractors** - In most cases, hiring long term independent contractors is the way to go.  You might pay a little more upfront in terms of their hourly rate but in the end you may end up saving yourself a lot of time and expense by not needing a full time payroll service or tax specialist, liability insurance, government contribution…..

61

**Disclaimer**: I am not a qualified legal counselor or a  financial advisor so please do your homework.  Legalities of doing business can change and it is your responsibility to validate any information from legitimate sources.

# PART 2  The PIE

The chapters in part 2 don't have any particular order despite the chapter numbers.  Every business has to have a round wheel to roll.  What I mean by that is that there are various areas within a business that are of equal importance and need their own special attention. If you don't manage them well you will experience a flat tire.  You can ride on it for a while but eventually you will do so much damage that the wheel will not be able to be repaired.

It is finally time to get into the joys of building your business, but if you are not careful your massive to-do list can quickly get out of hand. To avoid flat tires you are going to need a way to manage the workload and flow.

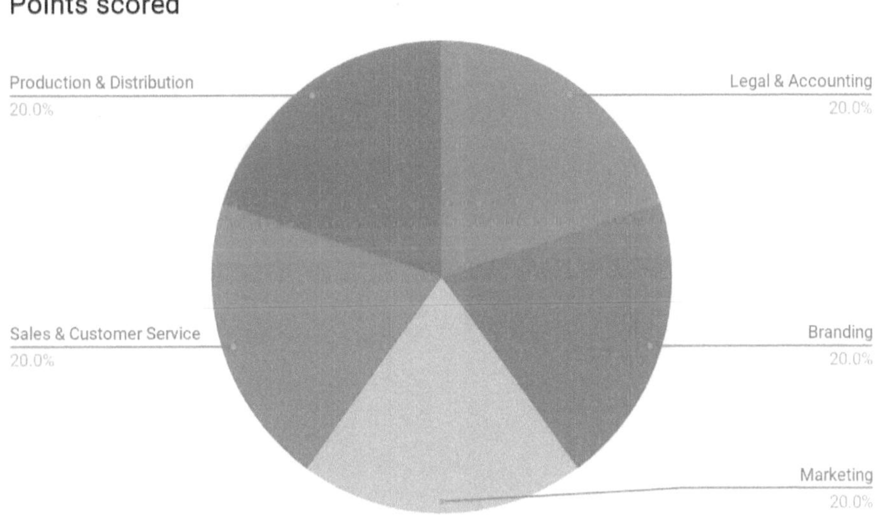

# Chapter 5

# WORKFLOW

### The Things We Focus On Tend To Grow

Are you like me? I try to be organized and I always start with the best of intentions but somehow life gets in the way. I lose my focus and forget where I'm at with all of the little tasks that need to be followed up on.

I was forever dropping the ball on little but really important things like a follow up sales call or fixing minor mistakes on websites. All stuff that can make you come across as unprofessional. I would also tend to take on too many tasks at once and then not be able to complete them properly.

This is a phenomenon that I also see with many of my clients. I think most entrepreneurs are creative people filled with great ideas and so much enthusiasm and that is a good thing. The problems start when that enthusiasm turns into too many projects that can not be managed and supported with the resources available.

Understanding that the job is not done until it is done, is an important lesson. Sticking to it until it is finished is going to take you further than starting and trying to manage too many things at once. I learned this the hard way and it cost me time and money that I could not afford.

For years I felt like a fraud, like I was bluffing my way through trying to convince people that I could handle their mandates but inside I was terrified that something would happen and I would fail to deliver what I promised. On occasion I failed miserably.

Most of the time the reason this happened was because I was not accurately assessing some very important key factors such as

1. The scope of the projects.

2. The resources of skill, time, and money to complete the mandates.

3. Tracking the progress and adjusting my approach to deal with delays and unforeseen events.

In 2012 I bought myself one of the best gifts, on GROUPON  of all places.  It was a course in Professional Project Management from IT University. If I remember correctly the course cost me $69. Learning project management changed the way I do everything and I now apply it to every part of my business.

I have worked with several project management systems but one that I really enjoy using is **Asana**. It is free for the basic functions and I can run multiple types of projects and have different accounts for different clients. It is a tool that lets me communicate with team members and keeps the conversations on the task.

Not everyone likes working with a project management system and I get it. I still work with my agenda and a notebook in front of me because I like the way I can jot stuff down without flipping through screens on my computer. Like I said earlier, I am easily distracted so the less I move through websites and documents on my computer the more likely I am to stay on task.

Where project management systems are really interesting is that you can chart your completed tasks, keep you focused on what is pending and see if you are on schedule or if your schedule is becoming overloaded.  If you are managing team members you can also follow their workload.   This is a way of preventing burn out and avoiding delays before they happen.

They provide easy visuals that I find quick to understand and motivating. When I see tasks getting done and the communication flowing, it feels great!  I compare it to getting a pat on the back for a job well done. The system keeps me organized and accountable to my objectives. This type of tracking helps me to feel more in control of my business and motivates me to do more.

Before learning project management and finding the right tools I was always worrying about what I might be forgetting and I could easily get myself into an anxiety spin that would sabotage my energy and motivation. I was constantly running a checklist in my head and it was exhausting.  Now when a good idea comes up I add it to the project management system.  It is given a priority and a time frame.  The system reminds me of my daily tasks,  so now I have more undivided attention for the task I am working on.

Most businesses are multifaceted even if you are the one doing everything. You need to think about your marketing, accounting, social media and whatever is involved in getting your product or service to your end user. A GOOD project management system allows you to manage and stay on top of business regardless of your business model.

Online software as a service (SAAS) providers such as Asana are becoming very intuitive and simple to use, and can be an affordable solution compared to having several managers and staffers. They allow you to manage and track work that can be easily outsourced to independent contractors. The perfect example of this is a social media marketing contractor, video editors, blog writers, websites developers...

You can invite each one of these people to work on your workflow system in their own project category while limiting their access to the rest of your business.  You can both upload documents, ask questions, share links and set due dates.  You each have your own unique dashboards that let you receive notifications and monitor progress in real time.

The other real advantage is that it helps you to break down the work flow into smaller tasks that are easier to complete and or to delegate to your team. The more tasks you have and the more people you have the easier it is to lose track. That is why project management systems are quickly becoming an essential part of even the smallest businesses. I can not recommend them enough.

Unless you are managing huge projects I don't think you need to take a 6 month course like I did, though it never hurts. There is enough information on the web and YouTube tutorial to teach what you need to know. With a little bit of dedication and a day to practice, I believe most people can learn enough to benefit from it.

Common Features of a good project management system are:

- Calendar
- Task assigner designation
- Due Date
- The ability to attach documents
- Invite team members to follow
- Text communicate with in the task
- Status update

- An app for your phone so that you can stay in touch with your team wherever you are

These are the features I use most. The nature of your business might require more specialty features so it is worth shopping around for the one that is the right fit for you.

One thing that is true is that good workflow management can reduce running cost and increase productivity and not to mention team confidence. When the people you work with can work well with you they tend to be more productive and enjoy the feeling of accomplishment that comes from a successful project.

A happy team means less staff turnover, less time wasted time hiring and firing and more time celebrating the successes.

At the beginning of the book I mentioned that I set out to write this book in 24 hours.  I am pleased to say that I wrote it in 22 hours.  That is all due to proper project management.  I figured that I wanted to write a book that would not be too long. I broke the project down into 4 phases.

1. Determining my subject and creating the outline
2. Writing the opening and closing paragraph for each chapter
3. Filling in the body of each chapter
4. Rereading my work and making sure I covered the key points of the book as simply as possible.

That does not mean the book project was totally complete in 24 hours.  But the part that relied on my writing was broken down into logical bite sized steps and executed according to my available time. Overall the book took 22 hours over 5 days to write.

I started this book project on June 11th and finished it on June 25th 2020

Writing, editing, copywriter graphic design and published in 14 days

A good workflow and project management challenges but does not overwhelm.

# Chapter 6

# BRANDING & MARKETING

**Branding is who you are.  Marketing is where you show  off.**

When I first started out, I knew nothing about branding and marketing or how important it is.  Fast forward almost 20 years and my <u>Hand Jam</u> bottles have changed quite a bit but I have kept core elements so that my loyal customers can easily recognize it despite the image upgrade.  Hindsight is 20/20

It might seem like a big and expensive job best suited for a swanky marketing firm but really it's not as complicated as it might seem.

**Branding** is really about presenting a unified image for your product or service that connects with your target market. This includes finding the right name and catch phrase that best describes your business. It should speak to your target market by promoting a core value of your company. Your name and catch phrase need to say it all. It needs to be clear, catchy and to the point. Here are 2 examples:

1. Pronto Edits - Fast Affordable Editing
2. Best Buds - Quality Plants & Flowers

Next comes your colour theme and logo design, their job is to visually  convey who/what you are and what you stand for. There is a lot of psychology behind colour and all of the big marketing firms know this. There are also colour trends within various business sectors. Before you decide on the key colours of your logo and branding, take a moment to write down the key words and feelings associated with your product or service. What message do you want to convey without using words?

Here are 2 logos made to match the examples above. They were made using logomaker.com's free online design tool.

1.  Fast Affordable Editing

2.  Quality Plants & Flowers

Wix.com offers logo making software, a free domain name plus a whole bunch of great add ons with their hosting service.  This one stop shop helps streamline the process of getting you up and running quickly.

Logo Design can be anything from initials, a stylized signature, simple shapes or designs that denote your business.

There are a lot of options to choose from. I recommend that you stick to customer expectations for your industry, like scissors for hairdressing or a paintbrush for an artist.  Something that says "This is what I do".

Your name, logo and catchphrase need to be everywhere your clients are and your design needs to be adaptable for your website, social media share, business cards, print material such as pamphlets, banner flags, trade show booths… be sure to get your logo in both high ( 300 DPI) and low (72 DPI) resolution.

Here are 2 books I recommend to help you with your branding.

1. The book, **<u>Introduction to the impact of color in advertising, marketing, and design: Psychological impact of color (Color psychology In marketing)</u>** is a good reference to give you the key principles of color applications.

2. The Book " **<u>Crushing it!</u>**: How Great Entrepreneurs Build Their Business and Influence-and How You Can, Too, Is a great book about creating your personal brand. This book talks about branding yourself not just your company and when it comes to working from home, this personal approach to branding is really important.  I think it is worth the time to read. You don't have to be obsessed with becoming a business superstar to learn and use the techniques outlined in the book to your advantage.

**Marketing** is about getting your name out there in front of your potential customers. Cold calling, mass email marketing and expensive newspaper ads are low impact approaches that eat up all your time. Unless your target market is seniors and you offer a service like appliance repair, downsizing or professional appraisal.

Generally seniors over the age of 75 are not comfortable with technology and rely on their children to help them navigate things like business listings, social media and video calling.

Everything is online now, so that is where you need to be.   It is tempting to try and build an audience using social media ads, but this can add to your frustration and expense if you don't have a solid plan.

Going back to "how simple can I make this". Here are some cost effective tips to get you visible on line ASAP.

1. Get your website registered with the major search engine and make sure your sites SEO is well done. WIX.com walks you through this process.
2. List your business with google map, Canada 411, TripAdvisor, Facebook, Pinterest, Linkedin and any local business directories, that might be popular in your community.
3. Look for local events that are being announced through Facebook and go with the intention of meeting people, or better yet plan your own local event related to your business.
4. Join online groups or associations related to your business. For example I am a member of several gemology and Jewelry groups, women in business groups, parenting groups… Some groups will let you promote yourself while others are strictly no selling. Either way it will help you grow, by helping you to understand your potential clients better.
5. Encourage customers to leave a review of your service.

Your online presence should tell people what you are offering and where they can get it along with a way to contact you, just like a business card.  The added advantage is that you can do so much more with your online presence than a business card.

Here are 2 examples of low cost effective branding and marketing:


1.  <u>Hand Jam Callus Care</u>.


You can find it online and learn about the product but really it is through the climbing community that this product continues to be promoted and shared.

We coined the term " <u>Jam Session</u> " to be that time of day where climbers gather around the campfire, maybe someone pulls out a drum or guitar, but mostly everyone talks about their days successes and defeat at the cliff,  Hand Jam is passed around and everyone soothes their sore hands.

We have deliberately emulated the van life, surf, snowboard and 420 culture as it is something that many of our users embrace as part of their chosen lifestyle.

Hand Jam is more than just a callus care product. It is about the making of memories and that shared experience that keeps the product in the hearts and minds of its users. Our website and social media is not just there to help point people to our point of sale but to remind our users that we are part of their community. The end of the day Jam Session is a shared ritual that is reinforced with an emotional high of a day well spent doing something you love. Hand Jam Callus Care at the end of a hard day work helps you to be in shape to do it again tomorrow.


    2. <u>Too Fat Too Loud Too Ambitious</u>, book site.


This site like hand jam was designed to point potential clients to the point of sale but it's also there to gather email contact information for those who want to be informed of any book signing dates, special video releases by the author as well as be informed of any new publishing. The site goes a step further to promote **<u>SexyBrilliant.org</u>**, the author's non-profit site dedicated to dispelling toxic shame due to addiction, body shaming, gender, sexuality, race, religion. The organization promotes radical self acceptance. The **<u>SexyBrilliant.org</u>** site takes you to her radio show, Dear Devina on Montreal's MikeFM. This is a web presence that is based on the concept of cross promotion. Cross promoting does not have to be expensive unless you are paying someone to do it all for you.



**Online or off,** I am a firm believer that word of mouth marketing is the best way to sell any product or service. It turns out it is also one of the cheapest ways to promote your business. Nobody can sell you better than a satisfied customer. Set the example by referring to people and companies that you really like and enjoy dealing with. As the saying goes "We get what we give!"

One of my first successful businesses was a beauty salon. I started out renting a table inside a busy beauty salon. I built my clientele by offering a free manicure to anyone who was having their hair colored.  After the service was complete, I gave them a business card with a 25% off coupon printed on the back valid for their next visit or they could give it to a friend.  They had 30 days to use it.

Within 3 months I was booked solid, and within a year I had opened my own day spa at a new location. This is the most I ever spent on marketing.  The total cost of this marketing campaign was the cost of the business cards and the sign on the front door.

The keys to a good marketing campaign is 3 fold.

1.  A low cost free sample know as a lost leader
2.  A time restricted deep discount offer.
3.  Offer 5 star customer service.

Where the number 3 also applies is in creating customer loyalty. Many studies show that if a client uses your product or service 3 times, they are more likely to continue using your product and services over time despite competitor promotions. This is especially true in the personal service industry. These relationships are also built on trust and the interpersonal connection. Take for example the local handyman, hairdresser or housekeeper. You don't want just anyone in your personal space.

When I owned my day spa I ran a permanent promotion. When you prepare 3 services and booked them in advance you get the forth one for free. My clients loved this because I was so busy. It was a way for them to guarantee their spot.

**SPECIAL PROMOTIONS** should be offered to fill in the gaps of your business. For example if you run an at home car wash company and Monday is your slowest day, then offer a Monday Special.

**BUILD AN EMAIL LIST** by asking people to sign up for special offers or newsletter, a chance to win xyz, to receive a discount. Admirers of your work will be the first to sign up and the first to toot your sales horn. These are your dream clients and It almost always pays to show them the love and appreciation they deserve with special communication and offers.

**CREATING A VIRAL FOLLOWING ONLINE.** This is where eyeballs count (online followers) This approach is perfect when your product or service is something like software as a service, or you've created an online course that addresses a major section of the population.  It also counts when you are relying on affiliate programs or selling advertising.

If traffic is the key to your sales strategy then you will need to use SEO strategies, engaging graphic design and video editing techniques to capture and keep attention on you. Today's audience has a very short attention span and it is getting harder and harder to impress the online community.

There is a lot of psychology that goes into marketing and the key is to create a visual, written and relevant campaign that plays on the heightened sense of emotions of your target audience.

By tapping into people's curiosity, fears, frustrations, sadness, laughter, love, joy. You will capture their attention. This can be done with bold fonts, the right use of color, dramatic facial expression and catchy titles.

At the heart of viral marketing is compelling storytelling. A story can be told in a single post in just a few words, through a simple visual, or a quick video. It can also be more drawn out such as in a blog, vlog or podcast.  There are so many ways to connect. My advice is to pick one to start and stick with it until you have mastered it, then automate that process. From there tackle the next platform and so on..

People connect through storytelling and every business needs a compelling story to draw in and  motivate the buyer to click the buy now button or say yes to your seasonal snow removal service.  There are many tools available to help you do this. Wix.com offers many tools and add-ons that can help you build a sales funnel that includes social media graphic design, sales forms, stock images, automated responses... They also offer a live chat feature so you can connect directly with site visitors in real time.  The built in analytic lets you see what type of devices your visitors are using, where they are coming from (Facebook, \ Linkedin ...) Which blogs are getting the most likes? All these little details help you to tailor your campaign for optimal results.

At the back of the book I will list additional resources for creating video intros, outtros, graphic design generators for social media, video editors, storytelling basics reference guides, blog formula reference guides ....

**A/B testing** is a great way to protect your marketing budget. Before spending major money on a marketing campaign it is a good idea to do a/b testing. This is a technique that many top ad agencies use before launching a major campaign. They create 2 OR 3 ads and run them back to back to a small group of people who represent the  target market. They then measure the click through response, for example, how many views each ad got, how many clicks and how many sales did each generate.

Typically they will continue to tweak the campaign until it is achieving optimal results before committing a long term promotional budget.

To successfully do a/b testing you must establish a way of measuring the results.  Again <u>wix</u> has a form builder app  so you can create custom questionnaires. Built in analytics go a long way in helping see what is working and what is not.

Here is an example of A/B Testing I ran for Too Fat Too Loud Too Ambitious.

**Step 1.**  I made 5 book covers and asked Devina's team to vote on them and we managed to narrow it down to 3.

# And the winner is...

Which cover do you love.
We need your vote.

**Step 2.**  We put the covers on line and asked her site members
to vote on them.  This narrowed it down to 2.

# And the winner is...

A        or        B

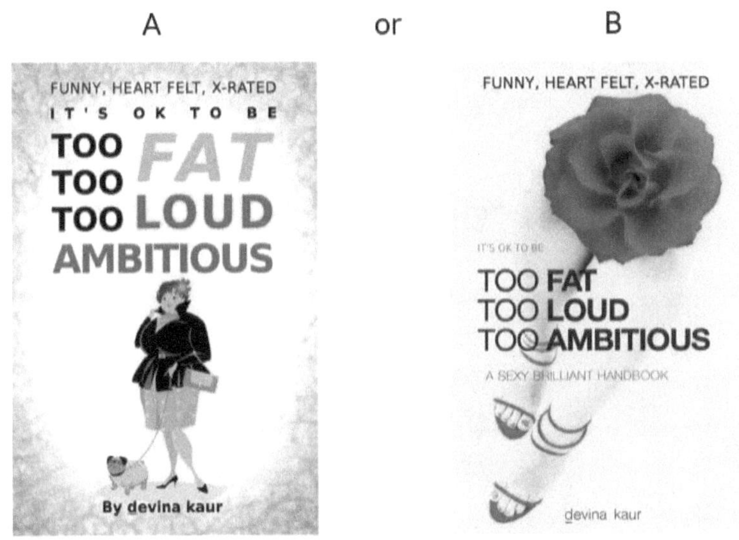


Which cover do you love.

We need your vote.

**Step 3.** I took the 2 printed book covers and did a tour around
North  America and asked real people to rate the covers. This
narrowed it down to 1.

Too Fat, Too Loud, Too Ambitious has been an insightful journey to self-acceptance and self-knowledge. The book offers an intense, open and honest perspective into Devina Kaur's biography and acts as the first x-rated self-help book. My favourite excerpt from the book is about marrying yourself and making a commitment to loving yourself and taking care of yourself for the rest of your life.

Jade, South Africa

Branding and marketing should reflect what you are selling eg. product/service, what you stand for and connecting with your target market . Focus on one campaign/platform at a time and track your results before going all in with a big budget. Follow these simple principles and you should be able to create a solid brand with a solid sales strategy.

Regardless of your online or offline platform, Facebook, snap-chat, YouTube, Pinterest, trade show booth, mailer, billboard, your goal is to find and or create your window of opportunity. To learn more about this

concept check out this Harvard's Business School article, <u>The Three Windows of Opportunity</u>

# Chapter 7

# PRODUCTION

**Work With What Works!**

If you are going the manufacturing route, you will  need to invest in inventory, have production space, and storage space for your finished products.  When working from home this can produce some obstacles.  If you have kids at home while you are working this may be a recipe for disaster depending on their age. Kids are notorious for getting into things when your back is turned. They can distract you at the worst possible moment and let's not forget that they often want to help.  I'm not trying to discourage you.  In fact I think that you can use your business as a teaching opportunity for your kids and they can be a part of the family business and company's success.

 People love kids and in the "New Normal Work From Home" business culture you are in good company.

My kids help me label bottles of Hand Jam. My daughter is great in English and reads through a lot of my writing.  I don't just ask for their help to keep them busy, I also really value it.  I struggle with dyslexia so having someone who can spot my mistakes saves me so much time.  It is a way to make them a part of the team and earn some extra cash in a way that is not cleaning the cat litter, or making their beds.

Whatever your plan is, make sure that you can manage the production within your available space, time that you can maintain quality control.

Recently a friend of mine, Claudette Lacasse from Au Coeur De Mes Passions started making ear protectors for nurses, so their masks would not irritate their ears.  Her base product and tools can be rolled and stored on a shelf or in a drawer very easily. She is able to make them in her spare time.

This is my idea of a simple idea that serves its community and is easy to execute with minimal investment, and minimal space requirements.  Her base product is easily sourced from local signage, craft  and office supply companies.  She produces on demand so there is no need to house her inventory for more than a few days.

Thinking about your manufacturing steps is important because when you work from home you sometimes need to take over your kitchen table or living room floor while in production.  A simple production process  helps you work efficiently and maintain quality control.   Having a dedicated space to store your supplies, tools and inventory, will also go a long way in keeping your house a home, when you are not at work.

The key things you need to figure out when manufacturing in
your home.


1.  Storage for your tools and supplies
2.  Production space
3.  Packaging and shipping


**DISCLAIMER**:  if you are considering producing food or cosmetic
products there may be inspections required before you can
legally sell to the public.  Be sure to inform yourself of any safety
precautions and regulations that must be followed as well as
informing the proper authorities. <u>Health Canada</u> should be able to
answer most of these questions for you.


Remember to ask yourself "how simple can I make this?"  and do
what is doable!

# Chapter 8

# ACCOUNTING & TAXES

## The Health Of Your Business Depends On it

The entrepreneurs NIGHTMARE! There is nothing creative about accounting and taxes unless you are planning on being a mobster or dedicated to retiring in a country with no extradition. It is entirely possible to find yourself in hot water with the government and your business partners just the same, even if you are an honest Joe.

Doing your accounting and taxes can be confusing and tedious and many people avoid it until it becomes a hellish job.  That is why I highly recommend figuring out your accounting system from the get go.  By scheduling regular moments in your daily, weekly and monthly to-do list you never fall too far behind and it is easier to stay on top of it.  You also avoid nasty surprises.

My business is very straightforward and is based on invoicing and monthly sales statements. Funds are deposited directly into my account.  My overhead is minimal in terms of products and office supplies, so that is also easy to track.  The hardest thing I need to do is fill out an expense report for specific projects.

I use a spreadsheet because my setup is ultra simple but there are a lot of great apps that will automate your accounting for you.  One of the best known is probably quickbooks. They let you scan receipts, write checks, calculate, GST and PST or HST, manage invoicing and more.

I have used it with several of my clients simply because they needed to track complicated spending from multiple accounts and trace receivables from multiple sources.

If you are a DIY type, and you feel like you are up to the task, again Groupon is a great place to find affordable courses on basic bookkeeping.

If your business is a bit more broad in scope then you at very least should consult with a professional book keeper  or a CPA to get you started on the right foot. Have them handle your general reporting to the government.

Depending on the size of your annual sales this could be only once a year all the way up to once a month.  The frequency is usually determined by the government after your first year of business and is based on the previous years business.  If you do not stick to your reporting schedule you may be penalized.

The last thing you want is to get into trouble with the government for back taxes owed or lose track of your bottom line. So do your homework and stay on top of it.

Remember, your accounting takes time and it is important.  Not doing it properly can have huge ramifications on your business. Avoiding it should never be considered a solution. When you don't stay on top of it, the cost of hiring someone to make sense of the mess can be exorbitant. It saves you a lot of time and money by starting on the right foot and setting up a simple method that is appropriate for your business.

I am not qualified to give professional advice when it comes to accounting and finances, but I am qualified enough to tell you, all too often we get busy in the doing and the creating that we lose sight of the maintenance of our business.

Years ago I worked at an IT firm and they did not set up their accounting from the get go. They started it but never followed up or maintained it.  They just jumped right in to doing what they did.  They were excited about all of the money they were raking in with some sweet high profile clients. Money was spent on new computers, expensive lunches and employees were hired all without a thought to the bottom line.  When it was time to do their end of year, they let that slide too.  When they finally got around to looking at the numbers, they owed the government almost 30,000 in various taxes, related to employee deduction, GST, and penalties for late filing.  None of that money had been set aside.

For a while, everyone tried to pass the buck and point finger placing blame, rather than taking responsibility.  At the end of the day no matter who's fault it actually is,  the boss ends up holding the bag.  You can't blame anyone but yourself if you are not staying on top of what is happening in your own company.

It took them well over a year to dig themselves out of the hole. The good news is that when they finally hired a professional to fix the mess,  they discovered that they qualified for research and development grants and they got back a nice chunk of change that helped to pay back the debts.

Needless to say the partners of the company each went their separate ways, and the company is no longer in business. The lesson here is that   a business can't run on talent alone. You need solid back office support and disciplined maintenance of that support to keep your foundation solid.

The sooner you set up your accounting system the better off you will be.  It is always a good idea to consult with a qualified professional if you are unsure of the legal requirements and how to do your declarations to the government. Pay now for the right information and avoid paying fines and penalties later. It is worth it!

# Chapter 9

# DELEGATING

### Leave Room In Your Day For Creativity

To hire someone might seem like a simple solution as opposed to cutting yourself in 2. Before you decide to bring someone else on board there are several factors to consider.

1. What is YOUR time worth vs how much should it cost to hire someone else to do that particular task.
2. Is it worth hiring someone with experience, versus training then from scratch?
3. Is it easier to outsource to a contractor versus having someone in house?
4. Can this person do it better than you and what is the expected result that can be translated into financial returns?

To hire well take a genuine understanding of the skill set and attitude needed for the position.  You also need a realistic understanding of the time required to do a job and adjust your expectations accordingly. Learning the various aspects of your business helps you to grow as a manager.  Once you start hiring you are essentially giving yourself a promotion to manager.

Management skills and a well orchestrated team are crucial for any growing business.  As an Entrepreneur you are the captain of your ship. The ship will sink or sail under your command.  In several HR studies it is proven that most qualified people leave managers not the work required of them. It is also shown that a good work environment and diversified team increases a company's productivity and success.

Key team players will even stay with an organization despite less pay if their top 3 needs are met (see chapter 1). It's not all about money.   In the book <u>Results at the Top</u>, Their research shows that a diverse team made up of men and women from different backgrounds, offer fresh perspectives on problem solving.  An inclusive environment also helps to promote psychological safety and this is a key component to building a strong team.

By operating with transparency and holding regular progress meetings your team will become focused on the goals and more proactive in supporting each other.  This has been proven to be a much more effective strategy compared to delegating tasks and demanding results.

So when is it time to hire?  This is a difficult leap for a lot of entrepreneurs after all for many of us our business is like our baby. It can be hard to trust someone to do the job the way we think it should be done.  The other issue that happens all too often is that we get too busy to be able to train someone properly.

The right time to start hiring is as soon as possible.  You don't necessarily need to take on employees but you should outsource as much of the work as possible to people who can do the job better and cheaper than trying to do it all yourself.  It can take time to develop a good team but once you do, the results will be well worth it.

A good team can create better quality ideas, come up with more creative solutions and make working less stressful.  The sooner you learn to become a good manager the faster you will have a profitable company that can grow.

Not every business needs employees, but the truth is we can not be good at everything.  From time to time it is worth working with people who have a particular skill or talent that you don't.  It's not a flaw to not want to be good at everything.  Just remember that when you expand your team you need to expand your managerial skills.

# Chapter 10

# OPTIMIZING

### The Key To Freedom

Once you get all the pieces of your business moving smoothly, looking into ways to streamline the process is a good use of your spare time. If you don't have spare time you NEED to ask yourself  "How simple can I make this?" With things running smoothly this is the perfect time to learn about optimization and refining your business skills.

If you are like me you might automate the entire process and find yourself with more time on your hands to come up with more creative ideas to share with the world. Or you might be the type to sit back and relax and enjoy the ride. Either way is perfectly fine.

Automating does not mean ignoring your business, or outsourcing all of it but it can mean that if you get the right systems working for you. Depending on your business model and the complexity of your systems, you may never be able to fully automate your business and that is OK.  If you love your work, clients and you thrive on the day to challenges of your career, then it is totally OK to stay in the thick of it, by mastering your skills you definitely gain a sense of pride in your work.

For me automation isn't about robots, and computers, though they have their place.  It is about streamlining the workflow.  Like greasing the bearings to improve the performance of your old washing machine.

It's about looking at every step of your process and finding the elegant solution.

I sell jewelry on Etsy.com and it is a good little side hustle. I broke it down into easy steps and created a simple routine. It goes something like this:

**Step 1**: Photograph the jewelry (3 photos for the Etsy store and one photo with the item on a piece of paper that had the inventory number on it), then place it in a well padded envelope with Thank You! cards and a discount coupon for their next purchase. Seal the envelope and write the inventory number on it. Then place the envelope in a file folder box with the inventory number facing forward.

**Step 2**:  Upload my images onto Etsy and fill out the product information detail and price.

**Step 3**:  Visit my Etsy store once a week to follow up with people who added my products on their wish list and send them a thank you for liking my item and offer them a 10% discount coupon.

**Step 4:**  Schedule all of my shipments for Monday and Fridays mornings followed by updating the tracking numbers in the etsy system.

**Step 5**: Answer incoming questions and follow up with the buyer to see how they like their purchase.

Some examples of how I streamlined this process are.

1. Buying branded envelopes, thank you cards in bulk saves me the trip of having to run to the store every time I ran out. It's also cheaper.
2. I take the time to personally write, Thank you for your business and sign my name in each card.  I typically do 100 cards at a time so they are ready when I need them.
3. Printing the inventory number on labels and having them ready for new inventory.  Before I did this by hand.
4. I now take the 4th picture directly on the numbered envelope.  This saved paper and a little bit of time.
5. I buy prepaid shipping envelopes from Canada Post, so now I just need to walk to my mailbox in the morning, while walking my dogs.

These may not seem like big or important changes, but all these little tweaks over time add up and the result is a smoother more enjoyable business that is low on stress, not to mention the added bonus of cost reduction and increased professionalism.

Hand Jam Callus Care is produced in batches a few times a year.  We call these our production days.

On these days our production space is cleaned from top to bottom, the formula is produced, bottled and labeled.  We don't stop until the production run is done.  For 2 days, life stops and the work marathon begins.

The lunch and supper menu is pizza, we run movies in the background as we get into the repetitive work of making sure the inventory is replenished.  Each step done to completion before starting the next.

1. Formulation
2. Bottling
3. Labeling
4. Bagging
5. Boxing
6. CLEAN UP. The job is not done until the clean up is done!
7. Shipping

My marketing is done by sponsoring athletes, Van Lifers, at local gyms, blogs and social media posts. I could make this business bigger by scaling production but honestly I  am quite happy being a bit of a cult niche product for now anyway.  It is important to me that **Hand Jam** never loses its grassroots feel.  Maybe one day I will expand it but for now I love it just the way it is.

By automating your business as much as possible, you give yourself space and time to be more in tune with the life you want to live.  Whether that be having more time with your kids, doing your favorite hobby, honing your skills or developing more creative ideas.  Workflow optimization is the gift of freedom that you give to yourself.  What you chose to do with it is totally up to you.

# CONCLUSION

No 2 entrepreneurs are alike, we have different personalities, needs, talents, interests, lifestyles and inspirations. The thing that every entrepreneur has in common is that we have a desire to sail our own ship towards our unique vision of what it means to be your own boss.

The most successful of us have a combination of talent, vision and discipline that we are able to harness into a product or service that people really need or want.

This new reality brought on by Covid-19 can be a curse but it can also be a wonderful opportunity to build a better life. A life that connects you with your talent and the people who can really appreciate it.

Starting your own business can feel like a daunting task and an empowering adventure all in one. By having a good sense of who you are and what is important for your happiness you will find a path that is best suited to you and your strengths.

When you couple your abilities and ideas with a solid business plan you have a blueprint for the road ahead. You will be better able to navigate the highs and the lows of business.

Treating each aspect of your business as a priority and managing it well with the proper tools, skills and people will make doing business easier and a lot more enjoyable for years to come.

There is no rule that says making money and working for yourself has to be complicated, oftentimes the simplest ideas are the most profitable and the easiest to maintain over time.  The more you focus on streamlining your workflow the less stressful your work will become.

Building a strong network of like minded people will help you to build your sales prospects and you never know where a referral will come from.  Set the example by referring to people and companies that you really like and enjoy dealing with. As the saying goes "We get what we give!"

I sincerely hope that this book offers some practical insight and guidance that you can use to tailor make the perfect, profitable, home based business that is just right for you.

Life changes and that is just a fact.  The more you embrace change the easier it is. The new normal working from home lifestyle may just be the opportunity that changes you for the better.

# REFERENCE INFORMATION

**BOOKS**

- <u>Principles</u> by Ray Dalio
- <u>Multiple Streams of Income</u> by Robert G. Allen
- <u>The Power of Now: A Guide to Spiritual Enlightenment</u> by Ekart Tolle
- <u>The Power of Habit</u> by Charles Duhigg
- <u>TOO **FAT** TOO **LOUD** TOO **AMBITIOUS**: A SEXY BRILLIANT HAND BOOK</u> by Devina Kaur
- <u>How to Sell Anything to Anybody,</u> by Joe Girard

**SALES REPRESENTATIVE OPPORTUNITIES**

- <u>**AVON**</u>
- <u>**TUPPERWARE**</u>
- <u>**EPICURE**</u>

**SERVICE PROVIDERS**

- **Wix** website builder—no coding skills needed. <u>WIX.COM</u>
- Selling on Amazon <u>https://sellercentral.amazon.ca/</u>
- Selling on Etsy <u>https://www.etsy.com</u>
- Selling on Fine Art America <u>https://fineartamerica.com/sell-art-online.html</u>
- Free Logo Creator, <u>Logomaker.com</u>

- Accounting with Quickbooks Quickbooks.com
- Standardizes Legal Forms Lawdepot.ca
- Asana Project Management  Asana.com
- Dreamstime - Stockphoto seller dreamstime.com


## OTHER:

- Myers-Briggs TEST- https://www.myersbriggs.org/my-mbti-personality-type/mbti-basics/
- Maslow's Hierarchy of Needs, https://www.simplypsychology.org/maslow.html
- Harvard's Business School article, The Three Windows of Opportunity
- Government Of Canada site: https://www.canada.ca/en/revenue-agency/services/tax/businesses/topics/registering-your-business/business-registration-online-overview.html
- ISBN Canada https://www.bac-lac.gc.ca/eng/services/isbn-canada/Pages/isbn-canada.a
- RS1 Canada - Bar-code Generation https://mygs1.gs1ca.org/self-registration-en
- BC Open Textbooks https://opentextbc.ca/principlesofaccountingv2openstax/chapter/calculate-predetermined-overhead-and-total-cost-under-the-traditional-allocation-method/
- BDC.ca https://www.bdc.ca/en/articles-tools/entrepreneur-toolkit/te

mplates-business-guides/pages/business-plan-template.aspx
- Health Canada Notification of Cosmetics https://www.canada.ca/en/health-canada/services/consumer-product-safety/cosmetics/notification-cosmetics.html
- Canada Food and Drug Regulation https://www.canada.ca/en/health-canada/services/food-nutrition/legislation-guidelines/acts-regulations/canada-food-drugs.html
- Canada Border Service Agency (Customs Tariffs and HS Codes) https://www.cbsa-asfc.gc.ca/trade-commerce/tariff-tarif/menu-eng.htm

**FOLLOW**

**NEW NORMAL - Working From Home & Loving It!**

**On Facebook & YouTube**

**https://www.facebook.com/NewNormalWorkingFromHome**

**https://www.youtube.com/channel/UCsc5hqgrwTPTdb7HDjgaSIA**